Flying *from* Malone

BELFAST'S FIRST CIVIL AERODROME

by Guy Warner

First published 2000
This edition published 2012 by
Colourpoint Books
Colourpoint House, Jubilee Business Park
Jubilee Road, Newtownards, BT23 4YH
Tel: 028 9182 6339
Fax: 028 9182 1900
E-mail: info@colourpoint.co.uk
Web: www.colourpoint.co.uk

Second Edition
First Impression

Copyright © Colourpoint Books, 2012
Text © Guy Warner, 2012
Illustrations © Various, as acknowledged in captions

A catalogue record for this book is available from the British Library.

Designed by April Sky Design, Newtownards
Tel: 028 9182 7195
Web: www.aprilsky.co.uk

Printed by GPS Colour Graphics, Belfast

ISBN 978-1-78073-007-3

Cover illustrations: Mrs Pat Jenkins

The Author: Guy Warner is a retired schoolteacher, who grew up in Newtownabbey, attending Abbots Cross Primary School and Belfast High School before going to Leicester University and later Stranmillis College. He now lives in Greenisland with his wife Lynda. He is the author of some twenty books and booklets on aviation, and has written a large number of articles for magazines in the UK, Ireland and the USA. He also reviews books for several publications, gives talks to local history societies and has appeared on TV and radio programmes, discussing aspects of aviation history. He is a committee member of the Ulster Aviation Society – for more information about the Society please see: www.ulsteraviationsociety.org.

Foreword

Message from The Rt Hon The Lord Mayor Councillor Robert Stoker

I was amazed to discover that in 1924 at the beginning of the great civil aviation age, Malone Air Park was established as the first municipal airport in the British Isles and that its greatest supporters were the then Lord Mayor, Sir William Turner and Belfast City Council, who authorised the princely sum of £15,000 to be released to purchase the land necessary for the air park.

The advantage of air transport over other methods such as road and rail is speed of delivery. Today, we think nothing of jetting off to the States for a three day business trip for example, or of commuting to London on a daily basis. Since the 1960s the arrival of cheaper charter flights means that for many of us going on a foreign holiday usually means travelling by air.

Sadly the air park closed after only one year's operation. A bold effort, which for a short time placed Belfast at the forefront of civil aviation in the UK. As we approach another new century and a new millennium we draw inspiration from the courage and vision of our recent ancestors. In Belfast we have a proud tradition of innovation and technology, and so we feel that Belfast is about to "take off" once again with confidence in our future.

Councillor Robert Stoker
LORD MAYOR
13 March 2000

Foreword to Second Edition

It has taken less than 90 years for the Upper Malone/Taughmonagh district to become the heavily populated suburb of Belfast it is today, familiar to thousands of residents, commuters and people like me who visit it often for business or pleasure purposes. And yet, most of us know little or nothing about one unique aspect of its history that is the subject of this book – Malone Aerodrome, which was the first municipally owned airport in the United Kingdom.

Ironically, that is one reason why I was delighted when invited to contribute the Foreword to the second edition of this wonderfully revealing account by aviation enthusiast and historian Guy Warner, so beautifully produced by Colourpoint Books of Newtownards. Another is the fact that I was born in Liverpool, which was the destination of the first commercial flight that took place from Malone to Aintree, piloted by the redoubtable aviator Alan Cobham, on 30 April 1924 – well before I was born, I hasten to add!

Sadly, the lifespan of Malone Aerodrome was only about one year. Nevertheless, its brief history is no less remarkable for that and belies the courageous and sterling efforts to make a successful go of it by pioneering aviators such as Alan (later, Sir Alan) Cobham, visionaries and entrepreneurs like Belfast's Lord Mayor of the time, Sir William Turner. Why then, did it fail? Quite simply, it was ahead of its time but, as I know from my own experience, hope, determination and the questing spirit will win out in the end, as Belfast Harbour Commissioners proved with the official opening of Belfast Harbour Airport thirteen years later.

Dame Mary Peters DBE, LL,
Her Majesty's Lord Lieutenant for the County of Belfast
20 January 2012

Introduction to Second Edition

For A SHORT TIME in the mid-1920s, Belfast was at the forefront of the development of civil air transport in the British Isles. Spurred on by successful commercial flights to the RAF airfield at Aldergrove in 1921–23, in a far-sighted and adventurous move, Belfast City Council established the first municipal aerodrome in the United Kingdom – at Malone, within the city boundary. A fledgling air company, Northern Airlines, was encouraged to set up services to Liverpool, Glasgow, Carlisle and Stranraer. Famous airmen of the time including Alan Cobham and RH McIntosh numbered among the pilots. The first passenger, issued with ticket number one, on the inaugural flight to Liverpool on April 30, 1924, was Sir William Turner, the Lord Mayor of Belfast and an enthusiastic advocate of air transport. The following account is a tribute to the pioneers and innovators whose names deserve to be remembered and a commemoration of a bold effort that played its part in paving the way for the global commercial aviation network that exists today.

I am delighted that Colourpoint is reprinting this little book. It differs only slightly from the first edition in that some new information and a few extra photographs have come to light. It is, however, always appropriate to celebrate the achievements of those pioneers and visionaries who sought to enhance Belfast's commerce and industry with innovative ideas.

Guy Warner
Carrickfergus, March 2012

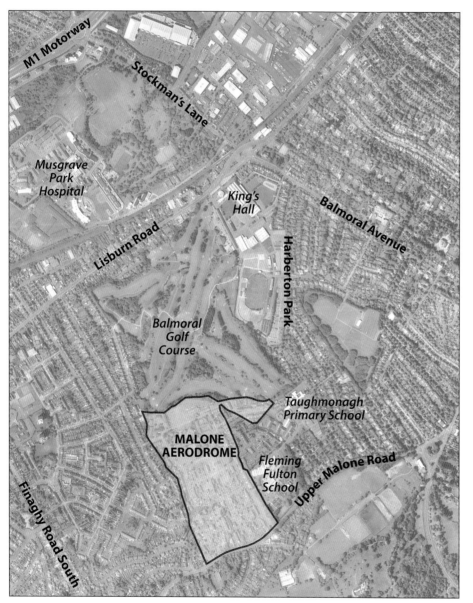

The site of the airfield at Malone in 1924–25 is shown here, superimposed on the local area as it appears today.

The Background

After the armistice of November 1918 brought hostilities to a close, there was an immediate surplus of military aeroplanes and pilots. Thoughts turned to their potential for commercial purposes. In England, the earliest airlines included George Holt Thomas's Aircraft Transport and Travel Ltd, which had first been registered as a company in October 1916 and started scheduled services in July 1919 from London to Paris with DH4s, DH9s and DH16s; the North Sea Aerial Navigation Co, which used the ungainly looking Blackburn Kangaroo to fly from Leeds to Hounslow and Handley Page Transport, based at Cricklewood, with the large O/400 ex-heavy bombers, for whom Lieutenant Colonel Sholto Douglas (who selected the site of Ulster's first aerodrome at Aldergrove in 1917) was Chief Pilot.

The machines were neither completely reliable nor very economical to run – being designed to fulfil the military needs of a short, hard, active existence. The pilots were by training and necessity both skilful and daring. Hard lessons were learned and it became apparent the air-routes which were most likely to succeed financially were those which required a sea crossing, where aerial navigation was quicker and more direct. It also was shown, particularly in the face of international competition from France, Germany and Holland, that government subsidy was necessary to promote economic viability and indeed survival. Hence, in April 1924, Imperial Airways was formed from the amalgamation of

Handley Page, the Instone Airline, the Daimler Airway and the British Marine Air Navigation Company, to act as the government's 'chosen instrument', with a policy to concentrate on international transport.

Early passenger flights to Ulster

The *Isle of Man Daily Times* of July 9, 1919 reported, "Major General JEB Seely CB, CMG, DSO, MP spoke in Belfast yesterday after flying across the Channel from Scotland in 14 minutes."

The only visit to Northern Ireland by the Avro 548 G-EAPQ in June 1921 (via Ann and Brian Stanley).

Avro 548 G-EAPQ landed somewhere on the outskirts of Belfast in June 1921. Posing amongst the onlookers are (l-r) Captain EDC Herne, AO Russell of Aero Films Ltd, and local man Andrew Stone, who would become Northern Airlines' Manager in Belfast (via Ann and Brian Stanley – Ann is Andrew Stone's niece).

The *Belfast Telegraph* added that he was one of five officers who flew over the city, the others being Brigadier General EL Gerrard CMG, DSO, Major Leslie DSC, DFC, Captain F Workman MC and Captain Gerrard. The accompanying photograph of one of the aircraft is somewhat indistinct but it looks very like an Avro 504. Seely was at that time the Under-Secretary of State for Air.

In June 1921 there had occurred what was described by *Flight* Magazine as a demonstration by the aeroplane "of its capabilities of playing an extremely important part in modern commerce." King George V and Queen Mary visited Northern Ireland to open its new parliament. Cinema newsreel cameramen and newspaper

One of the two DH16s, G-EALM, which landed at Aldergrove with a special edition of The Times *on December 5, 1922. (Author's Collection)*

journalists were flown over from England to record the event in four aircraft; two DH9s, the DH4A, G-EAMU and an Avro 548, G-EAPQ, proceeding to the RAF airfield at Aldergrove, where all the aeroplanes were serviced and refuelled. Pathé was able to show a film of the event in London cinemas that evening, while the national newspapers featured reports and photographs the next morning.

Eighteen months later, on December 5, 1922, a newspaper flight was conducted by two DH16s, G-EALM and G-EAPT, of the de Havilland Aeroplane Hire Service, bringing a special Ulster edition

Another view of one of the DH16s at Aldergrove in 1922. (Author's Collection)

Alan Cobham & Laura Stephens in front of the DH50, G-EBFN, 'Galatea', in which she had flown from Plymouth in September 1923. (Author's Collection)

Solomon Stephens emerges from the DH50, 'Galatea' at Aldergrove in September 1923. (Author's Collection)

Another passenger known to have flown in a DH50 from Belfast has been named as Elsie Irvine, seen here at Aldergrove. The man standing beside the pilot may well be Andrew Stone. (E Cromie Collection)

The experimental service from Plymouth of 1923 – Alderman William Turner is in the centre of this group at Aldergrove, with Alan Cobham behind, emerging from the cockpit of the DH50 G-EBFN. (Cobham plc)

of *The Times* to Belfast. This was followed in September 1923, by the trial of a postal service linking Plymouth, Birmingham, Manchester and Belfast, sponsored by the Air Ministry and the Post Office. It lasted for a month, using the DH50, G-EBFN. The Lord Mayor of Belfast, Alderman WG Turner was taken up for a trial flight over the city and became an enthusiastic advocate of the potential of commercial aviation. His pilot was the famous airman,

A cartoon featuring William Turner, October 1923. (Belfast Telegraph)

Alan Cobham, who commented, "The Lord Mayor became a convert to the flying game and convinced that Belfast must develop into an air port."

Newspapers were also flown from Manchester, with a DH9C, G-EBAX, being used, during the same period. They were then dispatched by vans belonging to Eason and Son Ltd to all parts of the Province. On October 16, 1923, the process was reversed, with the Belfast newspaper, the *Northern Whig* being sent to Manchester as, "the first Irish newspaper to try the experiment".

DH9c G-EBAX at Aldergrove in 1923 with a delivery of newspapers for Easons. (Easons Ltd)

Newspapers being loaded into an Easons van from DH9c G-EBAX at Aldergrove in 1923. (Easons Ltd)

Planning

An Air Ministry official, Noel Smith, had arrived in Belfast in connection with the Plymouth service and held meetings with civic representatives to discuss the future developments. He was of the opinion that Aldergrove was too remote from the city to be the ideal location for a civil air terminal:

> "It seems to me that the greatest need is a good landing ground as close to the city as possible. You don't want anything elaborate. You don't want sheds or anything like that. The aeroplanes could land passengers and mails at this ground in the city and then proceed to Aldergrove, which would be used as a base."

This had been the case in June 1921, when Alan Cobham had arrived initially "in a field near Balmoral where an aeroplane had once landed", off-loaded a quantity of *The Times* and had then flown to join the other three aircraft at Aldergrove for re-fuelling. Noel Smith was taken to inspect a possible landing ground at Balmoral and had commented that the ground had seemed a bit soft, especially for heavy aeroplanes. He added that the maximum dimensions of an airfield need be no more than 800 yards square and that pilots overflying the city had been instructed by the Air Ministry to keep their eyes open for likely sites.

Soon afterwards, it was reported in *Flight* Magazine that, on December 14, Lieutenant Colonel Francis Shelmerdine of the Air Ministry's technical department arrived in Belfast in the DH50, G-EBFN, *Galatea*, from Manchester, flown by Captain Walter Hope, to inspect an area of ground at Musgrave Park, "which the council propose should be provided for the purpose of a terminal point of the suggested air mail service between Belfast and Manchester." The

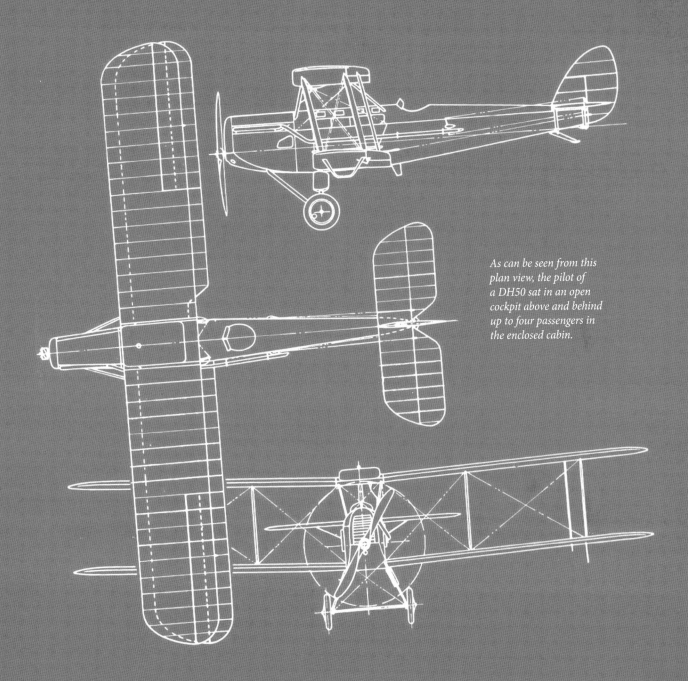

As can be seen from this plan view, the pilot of a DH50 sat in an open cockpit above and behind up to four passengers in the enclosed cabin.

Manchester airfield was Alexandra Park, which had been opened in 1918 and had been used by Handley Page Air Transport, the Avro Transport Co and the Daimler Airway. However, a fatal crash by the Daimler DH34, G-EBBS, on September 14, 1923, and the owner's reluctance to sell his land to the Manchester Corporation heralded the cessation of flying from this airfield.

Council Deliberations

First a suitable landing ground had to be established. In October 1923, the General Purposes Committee of the Belfast City Council had resolved as follows:

> "That in view of the advantage to the trade and commerce of the City which this committee are of the opinion would be gained by a regular air mail service, the Council be recommended to urge upon the Secretary of State for Air and the Postmaster General the desirability of the establishment of such a Service and further that the Council be recommended to give every facility for the provision of suitable ground for landing and starting."

Formal approval to proceed was given and so the visit of Colonel Shelmerdine took place. The *Belfast Telegraph* reported that Colonel Shelmerdine, his wife, Major Bartlett and Captain Hope were entertained to lunch by the Lord Mayor and the City Chamberlain, Sir Frederick Moneypenny, before proceeding to inspect the proposed site for the airfield. January 1924 saw a further step forward, when the Council determined, "in pursuance of the powers conveyed by the Air Navigation Act 1920 to establish and maintain an Aerodrome including the acquisition of suitable land and the erection of the necessary buildings together with proper apparatus and equipments." The sum voted for initial expenditure was £15,000.

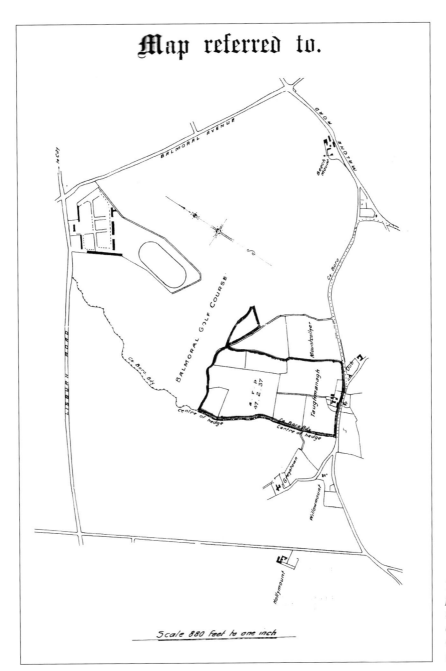

Map referred to.

Scale 880 feet to one inch

This map of the proposed site for the airfield was considered by the City Council early in 1924. (Belfast City Council)

By the end of the month a possible site had been identified on the Castlereagh Road – the Old Polo Ground. It must not be thought that the Council was carried away by enthusiasm, for the following prudent observation was made, "if the experimental air service does not prove a success, the land would always be useful for the purposes of a Public Park or for development as building sites."

A month later, Councillors were informed that negotiations in respect of the Castlereagh Road location had broken down – "owing to the price asked" – but that ground adjacent to the Malone Road had been identified as suitable. A plan was annexed to the minutes which clearly showed the location of the proposed aerodrome. The estimated costs were listed thus:

Approximately 36 acres @ £206:10:0 an acre

approx £7416

Approximately 7 acres @ £200:0:0 an acre

approx £1375

Agents Commission	£ 220
Removing hedges and filling ditches	£1000
Hangar	£ 700
Ground for road entrance	£ 250
Making Track	£ 250
Total	£11,211

A site is purchased

On February 22, Captain DM Greig was requested to commence negotiations for the purchase of the land at the Malone Road. The direct involvement of Donald Greig at this stage is significant.

Alan Cobham is on the right, the other pilot's name is not known. (Author's Collection)

Following service with the Royal Flying Corps in the Great War, during which he attained the temporary rank of Major and was appointed OBE, he became involved in civil aviation. He had been the manager of Aircraft Transport and Travel, and was a passenger on the first civil flight made on May 1, 1919 under the new Air Navigation Regulations. He had departed from Hendon in the early hours of the morning in the DH9, G-EAAA (C6054), with a cargo of newspapers destined for Bournemouth. Sadly this pioneer effort came to grief as the pilot, Captain HJ Saint, had to make a forced landing in fog on Portsdown Hill outside Portsmouth. Captain Greig also had been involved in the charter of aircraft in connection with the opening of Parliament in 1921. He was well known as a first class international tennis player, representing England several times, competing at Wimbledon and even becoming the singles champion of Poland. He was the runner-up at the Queen's Club Championships in 1922. He wrote *Lawn Tennis for Beginners* and was famous enough to be depicted on contemporary cigarette cards.

His doubles partner was Edward Higgs, with whom he won several European competitions and who also took part in the airline project, which was to become known as Northern Airlines. Initially the aircraft were provided by the de Havilland Aeroplane Hire Service, for whom the Chief Pilot was Alan Cobham – who not only was heavily involved in the early flights to Ulster but also was to become the most famous aviator in Britain over the next decade.

The bulk of the land, which was known as Taughmanagh, belonged to Mr Archibald Willis and he was willing to sell 47 acres for a price of £10,500, which brought the total cost to just over £14,000. The other landowner for the smaller parcel of ground was Mr John Thompson.

The Ministry of Home Affairs sanctioned a loan of £15,000 to go ahead with the scheme and the Ministry of Labour approved the use of 40 labourers under the Unemployment Relief Act to work on the preparation of the ground. The Air Ministry was asked for the free gift of a Bessonneau portable canvas hanger.

The last entry for March 27 provides a tantalising footnote, "Alderman Duff requested that facilities be given for filming the inaugural flights as a subject which might form part of an educational film to be produced for exhibition to school children and the Lord Mayor promised support to the proposal." If only.

During the month of April, preparations gained speed. A telephone connection was installed, trees blocking the approach path over the golf club were felled, telegraph poles on the roadway were marked by flags to make them clearly visible by the pilots, a 'First Aid Appliance' was organised and an application from the Anglo-American Oil Company was received, seeking permission to construct an underground petrol storage tank on the aerodrome grounds.

The Town Clerk wrote to the Air Ministry on April 25 in respect of the necessary operator's license, "under Article 7 of the Air Navigation Consolidated Order 1923, made in pursuance of the Air Navigation Act 1920", which was duly granted upon payment of a fee of three guineas (£3.15). Apparently this came from the Town

Clerk's own pocket, as he also applied for official reimbursement – which was approved.

Papers and Post

The primary idea in the formation of Northern Airlines was to accelerate the delivery of London newspapers in Northern Ireland, in which activity Eason and Son Ltd took the leading part as the major wholesale and retail newsagents in Ireland. However it was also intended to provide an airmail service and to carry passengers when the space was available. To this end, an arrangement was made with the Postmaster-General that airmail letters would be carried at a surcharge of one halfpenny and a single fare of £3.00 was set for the journey from Belfast to Liverpool only.

Flight Magazine dated May 1, 1924 carried the following announcement:

AIR MAIL SERVICE FOR LETTERS FROM BELFAST

The Postmaster General announces that on Thursday, May 1st, a new Air Mail will be instituted for letters etc., but not at present for parcels from Belfast to Liverpool. The special air fee will be ½d per 2oz. in addition to ordinary postage at the appropriate inland or foreign rate. The mail will be closed at Belfast Head Post Office each week-day at 5.35pm for packets posted in the public letter-box and at 5.45pm for packets on which an additional late fee of ½d per packet has been prepaid.

The following advantages are offered for packets posted in Belfast and most other places in Northern Ireland in time for inclusion in the Air Mail :-

(a) Earlier delivery generally in England (the North excepted) and Wales; and in particular, delivery by first post the next morning in London, Cardiff, Bristol, Nottingham and most other large towns.

(b) Connection with dispatches to the Continent from London next morning either by Air Mail (subject to additional prepayment of the relative air fee as shown in the Air Mail leaflet) or by ordinary route.

(c) Connection on Tuesdays and Fridays with the next day's regular dispatches to Canada, United States of America, etc., from Southampton (as shown by the Post Office Daily List).

The airfield selected in England was Liverpool, Aintree – on the racecourse – which had been used in 1918–19 for the test flying of Bristol Fighters built at the adjoining National Aircraft Factory No 3.

Shareholders in the company included, the Baird family (the proprietors of the *Belfast Telegraph*, Harry Ferguson Ltd (the firm belonging to Ireland's first aviator, who made his historic flight on December 31, 1909), Lord Londonderry (a keen airman and future Secretary of State for Air), Sir Thomas Dixon, Sir William Turner, as well as many local businessmen and mill owners.

Inaugural service

The first commercial flight from Malone was made by Alan Cobham on April 30, 1924 in the DH50, G-EBFP, to Liverpool but the sodden state of the ground that day, which rendered take-off more difficult was a portent of the troubles facing this venture. Cobham and the Director of Civil Aviation, Sir Sefton Brancker,

Sir Sefton Brancker at Malone. He is the third from the left with Alan Cobham just behind him. (Cobham plc)

had left Liverpool the previous day at 7.45am, arriving at Malone two hours and ten minutes later. A luncheon party was held at the City Hall, hosted by the Lord Mayor, now Sir William Turner. Those invited included, of course, Cobham and Brancker, as well the High Sheriff, Councillor Hugh McLaurin, Sir Thomas Dixon, Rt Hon HM Pollock, the Minister of Finance, Alderman James A Duff MP and Captain DM Greig. Press photographs of the event show a dark suited collection, heavily moustached, with homburgs and bowlers, spats and starched collars.

On the morning of Wednesday April 30, exceptionally bad weather put something of a dampener on the opening ceremony but a crowd had assembled to witness the first departure, which was delayed from 10.00am to 12.17pm. The Lord Mayor, in his inaugural address, emphasised that it was the expansion of commerce that was driving the venture:

> "When I was a boy, I was at a loss to know the meaning of the letters SPQR displayed by an enterprising tradesman. My inquisitiveness soon satisfied my curiosity, for I learned that the letters meant – Small Profits, Quick Returns – might the same letters now be adopted as the motto in connection with this new service but with a more modern interpretation – Swift Postage, Quick Replies."

The passenger list was restricted to the Lord Mayor and High Sheriff only, Sir Sefton Brancker and Alderman Duff standing down, a high weight take-off being regarded as unsafe in the prevailing conditions. The DH50 was a rugged and reliable aircraft but had only a single 230hp Siddeley Puma engine. It could carry four passengers in an enclosed cabin in front of the pilot, who was exposed to the elements. Passengers embarked by climbing onto the lower wing from the rear and then clambered past the glazed, hinged hatch cover down into their snug cabin behind the engine. The view to either side would have been partially obscured by the lower wing but the rectangular windows were relatively large.

The events of the opening day were covered in some detail in the Belfast News Letter. (Belfast Central Newspaper Library)

BELFAST NEWS-LETTER, THURSDAY, MAY 1, 1924.

BELFAST-LIVERPOOL AIR MAIL SERVICE.

The aeroplane starting on its flight to Liverpool from the Belfast Aerodrome yesterday. Inset—Major-General Sir Sefton Brancker (left) and Mr. Alan J. Cobham, the pilot.

Left—The Lord Mayor taking his place. Right—Spectators examining the machine.

Some of those present at the aerodrome, including the Lord Mayor and Lady Mayoress and their daughter, Miss E. Turner.

William Turner addresses the crowd at Malone on the opening day. Sir Sefton Brancker is to the left, wearing a monocle and holding his bowler hat. (Cobham plc)

Assembled guests pose in front of a DH50 at Malone. Note the opened hatch giving access to the passenger compartment. (Cobham plc)

DH50 G-EBFP prepares for departure from Malone. (Cobham plc)

Securing the passenger cabin of the DH50 G-EBFP before flight. (Cobham plc)

The Lord Mayor of Belfast (on the left) is welcomed by Sir Archibald Salvidge (on behalf of the Lord Mayor of Liverpool) at Aintree. The pilot, Alan Cobham and Hugh McLaurin, the High Sheriff of Belfast, look on from between and behind. (Cobham plc)

The contemporary report in the *Irish Telegraph* noted that:

> "A wireless station, speedily erected by the RUC platoon, opened communications with cross-channel stations to ascertain conditions along the line of the route it was proposed to follow. The Lord Mayor, who displayed the keenest enthusiasm in the proceedings, was most anxious that the flight from Belfast should, if not according to the timetable, at any rate be effected on the day selected."

Sir William Turner's readiness to lead by example can only be admired. After a difficult flight due to rain, wind and low visibility,

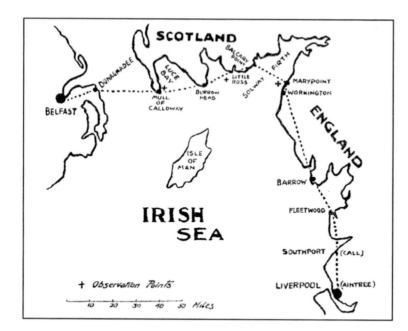

The route from Belfast to Liverpool and the waypoints in between are clearly shown on this contemporary map. (Author's Collection)

Liverpool was reached that afternoon at 2.45pm. The route taken was from Belfast to Donaghadee, then across the sea to the Mull of Galloway, following to Scottish coast eastwards before crossing the Solway Firth and passing over Workington, Barrow, Fleetwood and Southport. *Flight* Magazine noted:

> "a landing was effected to the accompaniment of hearty cheers from the crowd which had gathered at Aintree aerodrome. Pilot and passengers were officially welcomed by civic dignitaries and were subsequently entertained at luncheon in the Town Hall."

Sir William Turner addressed the lunch party:

> "My dear Lord Mayor, – I tender greetings to you and to the citizens of Liverpool on the occasion of the inauguration of the air-mail service between Belfast and Liverpool, which has taken place this afternoon and is the first venture of the

kind to be established in the United Kingdom. On such an auspicious occasion may I be permitted to convey to you and your citizens the good wishes of the people of Belfast and to express a hope that the ties of friendship between the great county of Lancashire and the capital of Northern Ireland will be strengthened by this new service."

Suitably refreshed, Sir William returned to Belfast by air, leaving Aintree at 5.30pm and landing in Belfast at 7.30pm. He still found time to send a telegram to the King and received the following reply:

"Buckingham Palace. – To Sir William Turner Lord Mayor of Belfast. – I thank you my Lord Mayor on the occasion of the inauguration of the daily air-mail service between Belfast and Liverpool, which I feel will be of great value to the general community. – George R.I."

A promising start

By the middle of May, *Flight* Magazine was able to report that the air service was proving to be a success and was booked up for several months ahead. It added that season tickets costing £50 for six months were being sold. The first regular air mail flight on May 2 had carried 1500 letters. As well as G-EBFP, another DH50, G-EBFN, was also used.

The City Council minutes of May 5 noted that as the requested hangar had not been supplied, it was necessary to rope off the aeroplanes while on the ground. Further evidence of a simpler age is provided by a report on the same page that, "in order to keep the grass as short as possible, it would be necessary to let a portion of the grounds for the grazing of sheep." Drainage of the area was

Belfast to Liverpool First Day Cover May 1924.
(via Jim Hamilton)

This view of DH50, G-EBFN, at Malone shows the location of the passenger accommodation ahead of the cockpit. (Cobham plc)

THE AIR MAIL SERVICE.

RECORD FLIGHT.

Belfast to Liverpool in Eighty-eight Minutes.

145 MILES AN HOUR.

Th aeroplane which carried the mails between Belfast and Liverpool last night accomplished the journey in the record time of 88 minutes, flying at a speed of 145 miles per hour.

The machine, which was piloted by Mr. Dickinson, left Malone aerodrome at 6-15 and landed at Aintree at 7-43. A large sack of letters and a smaller one containing registered packets comprised the mail, and in addition two passengers were carried, one of whom was Captain D. M. Greig, the organiser of the service. Three passengers had booked for the journey, but two of them were unable to travel.

The weather was very favourable for flying, visibility being about 50 miles, while there was a strong wind behind the aeroplane for the greater part of the route. Prior to the D.H. 50 leaving the ground Captain Greig expressed the belief that the trip would be made in record time, but when the wireless message giving the time of arrival was communicated to Mr. A. W. Horwood (Northern Air Lines) he endeavoured to verify it, and at 10-15 received a telegram from Captain Greig in confirmation. The feat is probably a record for a commercial aeroplane, though much higher speeds have been attained in competitieve events. The King's Prize last year was won by F. T. Courtney, flying at 150 miles per hour, while L. L. Carter, in the aerial Derby travelled at 192 miles per hour. The Lord Mayor (Sir William Turner), on receipt of the news of the flight, telegraphed his congratulations to Mr. Horwood.

Yesterday morning Mr. Dickenson left Liverpool at six o'clock, but was delayed at Southport and did not leave there till 7-20, arriving in Belfast at 9-15. Mr. Dickenson, who has been engaged in the London to Paris service, said the visibility over the Channel was fifty miles, and the conditions were ideal for flying.

The promoters feel grateful for the manner in which the public are supporting the venture, passengers having booked for various dates in the future, and it is anticipated that the enterprise will be a commercial success.

Northern Air Lines have issued what is probably the first season ticket, the holder being Mr. W. R. Boyd, Colenso Parade, manager of the General Electric Company. The price of the ticket, which was issued by Messrs. Eason & Sons, is £50, and it covers a period of six months. The number of these tickets to be issued is strictly limited.

BELFAST AIR SERVICE.

Heavy Mail Despatched to Liverpool Last Night.

THREE PASSENGERS CARRIED.

Despite heavy rain and low visibility, the mail aeroplane last night covered the distance between Belfast and Liverpool in a little over two hours, carrying, in addition to three passengers, the heaviest consignment of letters since the service commenced. The pilot was Mr. Dickenson, who in the previous evening had achieved a record flight, and the passengers were Sir Robert M____er, Town Clerk of Belfast; Mr. Frank Douglas, advertising manager of Messrs. Eason & Sons, Ltd.; and Mr. H. Barbour.

The mails arrived at the ground at 6-16 and were quickly transferred to the aeroplane, which left the ground a minute later to the accompaniment of the cheers of the large company of visitors. In consequence of the clouds and the pouring rain the pilot at first flew very low, but, travelling at a high speed, the 'plane was soon lost to view as it headed for the County Down coast. After the departure the weather became worse, and some anxiety was expressed as to whether it would have any effect cn the flight. All doubts, however, were set at rest when Mr. A. W. Horwood received a wireless message intimating that the aeroplane had arrived at Aintree at 8-30.

The value of the wireless installation erected at the ground by the Wireless section of the R.U.C. under Captain Campbell cannot be overestimated, and until the Air Ministry have erected a wireless station at the Malone aerodrome it is to be hoped that the service will be maintained. The Northern Air Lines recognise the great assistance that has been forthcoming, and are deeply indebted to the Northern Government, Colonel Sir Charles Wickham, Inspector-General of the Royal Ulster Constabulary, Captain Campbell, and Major Day, of the Royal Corps of Signals, for their co-operation and help in this matter, which has made possible the prompt receipt of weather reports from the other side of the Channel.

Captain D. M. Greig, the organiser of the venture, who is at present in London, is to be congratulated on overcoming many difficulties and on giving the citizens a very efficient air mail service. The business community have realised the benefits of the acceleration in letters to cross-Channel destinations, and the volume of correspondence being despatched nightly is growing larger. The Postmaster, Mr. T. B. M'Dowell, has afforded every assistance to the scheme, and Mr. Horwood, who was privileged to see the mail being sorted at the G.P.O. yesterday evening, expressed his admiration for the expeditious manner in which the work was carried out. Twenty-four letters which were posted after the stated hour were included in last night's despatch.

presenting a problem and the City Surveyor was tasked to take steps to rectify the matter.

The *Belfast Telegraph* of Thursday May 8, 1924 was very enthusiastic about the new service:

> "The Lord Mayor (Sir William Turner) has received many congratulatory letters from cities and towns in England on the success of the Belfast–Liverpool air mail service. These indicate numerous instances of highly important business letters, addressed by Belfast merchants having reached their destination hours before they could have been delivered under normal post conditions. The route is now being largely and increasingly availed of and there appears to be little doubt as to a permanent service being established."

Alan Cobham was then interviewed and commented in some depth on the practical and organisational matters in which he had been involved:

> "Mr Cobham, who is the chief pilot of the de Havilland Company, reached Belfast this morning with newspapers etc, after a two hours' flight. He states that he and his colleagues are learning more about the route day by day and that the organisation is becoming more and more complete, so that in a very short time the service will settle down into a regular routine. Everyone, he said, seems to be doing their little bit on the flying side without any trouble or difficulty. He acknowledged the public support already given to the enterprise and went on to explain that Northern Airlines was the customer of the De Havilland Air Craft Company who arranged on a contract basis to run a flying service between two points at a stipulated figure per trip. Mr Cobham has

charge of the flying end and in order to make the service regular, punctual, safe and speedy he has accomplished a great amount of spadework in acquiring the necessary wireless communications between the two centres. He has been greatly facilitated in this direction by the military and constabulary authorities. Now there is a definite promise from the Air Ministry to establish a permanent wireless station. In the original survey of the route, Mr Cobham had the invaluable assistance of Colonel Shelmerdine of the Air Ministry, particularly in the matter of landing grounds every twenty miles. Observation posts were also established and in this connection ready assistance was forthcoming. Indeed there were enthusiastic offers of help and Mr Cobham cited the case of a gentleman at Drummore – Mr M'Cracken, the proprietor of a garage there. This gentleman is a keen aviator and when he learned from the lighthouse keepers of the intended service he at once placed himself in communication with the promoters and has since furnished most valuable reports."

The article concluded with some advice to potential customers:

"It is emphasised that letters intended for the air mail should bear an additional half-penny stamp and also carry the official blue adhesive stamp, to be obtained at any post office or otherwise be distinctly marked 'By Air Mail'. Mr Cobham is quite convinced from experience that a regular service can be maintained. Passengers have been booked for tonight's journey."

The *Belfast News Letter* dated Thursday, May 8 carried the story of the first lady passenger, Miss Sarah Ingram, the departmental manageress of Messrs Eason and Son. Her flying companions were James A Duff MP and Reverend HG Maturin of the Seamen's Mission. The pilot was Alan Cobham and the party was waved off by the Lord Mayor. The intrepid Miss Ingram reported her experiences to the *Belfast Telegraph*:

"It was simply great and I enjoyed the flight tremendously. It was the smoothest journey I have ever experienced. The machine was much steadier than a motor-car. I dined on board with Alderman Duff and Mr Maturin, who were my fellow passengers." She also had the time and forethought to record a diary of the flight, "Left Belfast 6.14pm; passed over Donaghadee 6.22, quite a fine sight. Passed over Drummore (Mull of Galloway) 6.37, sighted Burrow Head 6.48. We then crossed Wigton Bay, saw Little Ross lighthouse and then flew over Solway Firth to Maryport, where I was told the machine was observed by the watchers. We came down the English coast, over Workington, Whitehaven and Barrow-in-Furness (Walney Island). It was now 7.40. We cross Morecambe Bay and here we sight the Blackpool Tower. It is a grand evening and as we fly over Blackpool, we can easily read the sign outside the Winter Gardens and can see the time by the Winter Gardens clock – it is 7.54. We reached Liverpool at 8.10."

Later in the month, Councillor Milan wrote to the General Purposes Committee, suggesting that:

"All Corporation deputations visiting cross-channel centres should, as far as possible, travel by the Northern Airline and that the company be approached with a view to a special reduced rate for such public representatives when travelling on public business."

Once more the local press took considerable interest. (Belfast Central Newspaper Library)

FIRST LADY PASSENGER

Travels by Air to Liverpool Last Night.

Carrying the first lady passenger to travel by air from Belfast the Northern Air Lines mail aeroplane left Malone aerodrome at 6-15 last night and arrived at Aintree at 8-10. The pilot was Mr. Alan Cobham, chief pilot of the De Havilland Company, and the passengers were Miss Sarah Ingram, departmental manageress, Messrs. Eason & Son, Belfast, one of the first to purchase a ticket for the new service; Alderman James A. Duff, M.P., and Rev. H. G. Maturin, B.A., of the Seamen's Mission, Belfast. The Lord Mayor was present when the 'plane left and congratulated Miss Ingram on being the first lady to make the journey.

The heavy hailstorm which swept over the district prior to the start rendered the surface of the aerodrome somewhat sodden, but despite the heavy load the D.H.50 took off beautifully and was soon well on the way to Liverpool. On arrival at Aintree Mr. Cobham despatched a message to Mr. A. W. Horwood giving the time of arrival, and stating that all the passengers had thoroughly enjoyed the experience. Alderman James A. Duff wired as follows to the editor of the "Belfast News-Letter":—

"All passengers delighted. Most interesting and enjoyable journey. Steadiest method of travel yet experienced by me. Time, 1 hour 55 minutes. Telegram of greeting received from Liverpool Lord Mayor."

Mr. Max Erard, who is appearing at the Belfast Hippodrome, took advantage of the air service to send a parcel of pictorial posters to Burnley, which he is to visit next week. This is the first goods parcel to be sent by the new service.

The Town Clerk (Sir Robert Meyer), who crossed on Tuesday, returned by steamer, leaving Liverpool at ten o'clock last night, and motored yesterday morning from Donegall Quay to Malone aerodrome, being present when the aeroplane arrived at ten minutes past eight. He said all the passengers enjoyed the trip on Tuesday night and did not have any rain after leaving Belfast. Sir Robert entertained Mr. Cobham and Mr. A. M. Stone, local manager, Northern Air Lines, to lunch at the Reform Club yesterday. Mr. Cobham stated that the coastal route from Liverpool to Belfast would prove practicable for flying, as this morning only two or three miles inland there was heavy rain throughout the journey, and yet all along the coast the visibility was twenty or thirty miles with a clear sky."

TRAVELLERS BY AEROPLANE.

ALDERMAN DUFF, M.P.; MISS INGRAM, REV. H. G. MATURIN, AND MR. ALAN COBHAM (PILOT),
WHO FLEW FROM BELFAST TO LIVERPOOL LAST NIGHT

The Belfast News Letter *featured the passengers and pilot described in Sarah Ingram's diary. (Belfast Central Newspaper Library)*

Charles Grey comments

A further, more detailed account of the service was given in the issue dated June 11 of the periodical *The Aeroplane*. This was a highly respected and authoritative publication, rendered all the more readable by the trenchant and uninhibited opinions of the editor and founder, Charles Grey (1875–1953). He began by praising the initiative shown in setting up a municipal aerodrome and by the sound business sense of a regular newspaper delivery contract underpinning the venture. Concerning the viability of a passenger service he wrote:

"One Belfast businessman whose business brings him to England every few days has bought a season ticket to Liverpool. He finds that an air trip for a couple of hours in the middle of the day, after he has done his morning's work in his Belfast office, is rather refreshing whereas the night journey by boat and train consumes energy. Others are already talking of following his example."

He then turned to the Malone airfield:

"The aerodrome at Belfast is situated to the South and a little to the West of the city about opposite Balmoral between the Malone Road and the Lisburn Road – which is the main road to Dublin. Although it is within a few minute's ride of the centre of Belfast by tramcar it is in very open country, especially towards the South and West whence the prevailing winds blow. Towards the North and East there is enough open ground to afford a safe landing in case an engine should fail when a machine is just leaving the aerodrome. Also there are no high buildings or trees to hamper the approach of a machine when landing from any direction. The enthusiasm created in Belfast by the new line is remarkable but quite understandable by anybody who knows the energy which a Belfast man puts into a job when once he is convinced it is worthwhile."

Grey then went on to detail the meteorological arrangements:

"There is no wireless station at Belfast aerodrome. Therefore, as it is essential that news of the Liverpool weather should be supplied to the pilots, the Belfast police provide the necessary mechanism. Every morning one of the constabulary with a mobile wireless outfit on an automobile goes out to the aerodrome and gets in touch with the RAF airfield at Shotwick in Cheshire. The RAF station telephones Aintree and asks what the weather is doing there and then reports to Belfast whether the machines will be able to start or not. Shotwick and the Belfast police between them do their best for the safety of the aircraft and up to the present results have been satisfactory."

He was much less enthusiastic about the facilities and enterprise shown at the Liverpool end:

"At Liverpool things are very different. The only available aerodrome is at Aintree, which is too small for a fully loaded DH50 to be sure of getting out of it under all weather conditions. Consequently the machines have to fly out of Aintree without their loads and land on the sands of the seashore at Southport, whither the newspapers have to be

RECORD AEROPLANE FLIGHT.

Mr. Dickenson, pilot of the aeroplane which carried the mails from Belfast to Liverpool on Monday evening, and covered the distance in 88 minutes, giving an average speed of 145 miles per hour.

Captain VM Dickinson makes the news. (Author's Collection)

taken by car from the railway station at Liverpool some 20 miles away. The Liverpool Chamber of Commerce seems to take no interest in flying and cannot see that it would be to the advantage of Liverpool to have an aerodrome worthy of the size and importance of the city. While others have talked about it Belfast has done it."

As well as Alan Cobham, the pilots on the service included Captain VM Dickinson and Lieutenant Colonel GLP Henderson. *Flight* Magazine reported that in seven weeks some 1000lbs of mail had been carried.

Problems

The hope and confidence expressed by Charles Grey was not to be realised and in the following edition of *The Aeroplane* he was obliged to report:

> "Northern Airlines have been compelled to suspend the Liverpool–Belfast air line. The weather conditions of the past few weeks made flying with the necessary regularity impossible. The stage along the South coast of Scotland has suffered from sea mist, morning fog and low clouds day after day and the clouds over the Lake District have been so heavy that pilots have been forced to make the detour by the coast. Frequently, pilots have taken the direct compass course over sea almost devoid of shipping as the only way of avoiding the low clouds over land and that is too dangerous to be permitted as a habit. In spite of this a 60% service has been accomplished which is very good. To make matters worse, the Air Ministry has, so one is told refused to co-operate with Northern Airlines in furnishing adequate weather reports. Also the Lisburn Road aerodrome (Malone) has become waterlogged and several times have had to take the machines to Aldergrove 15 miles from Belfast so as to get off with a full load."

A report in the *Belfast Telegraph* commented on the suspension of the air route:

> "It was emphatically denied by Mr Horwood of Messrs Eason and Son that the airmail service has been abandoned. It had merely been temporarily suspended. He added that seaplanes had been arranged for use as a stand-by..... though they not in themselves a commercial proposition.

When taxi-ing on the water their speed did not exceed 18 miles an hour and were exceedingly expensive. Landplanes could carry a load of 1000lbs, while seaplanes could not carry anything like that weight."

The Scottish connection

Undaunted, Northern Airlines tried another route – with the start of a daily flight to Renfrew airfield, Glasgow from the middle of June 1924. *Flight* Magazine noted in July that the Liverpool–Belfast air service had been discussed in Parliament:

> "Viscount Curzon asked the Under Secretary of State for Air why the service had been suspended and if it was intended to be restarted. Mr Leach replied that it had been discontinued because of the limited special weather reporting facilities and the bad weather rendered the service too unreliable to be economic."

It should be remembered that the operations of Imperial Airways at this time received considerable government subsidy, without which they also would have been uneconomic. The government did, however, install a Wireless Station consisting of a van, an aerial and also meteorological equipment, at the aerodrome. Part of the stable building was rented, at a cost of £3 per quarter, as an office for the radio officer, whom the Air Ministry also provided. The council's expenses were further defrayed by the sale of grass cut on the airfield and the grazing rights sold back to Mr Willis.

The *Glasgow Herald* dated June 17 commented at some length on Northern Airlines' plans and operating experience so far:

> "The probable decision to make Renfrew the connecting link

An interested crowd gathers around a DH50 at Malone. (Cobham plc)

for the air mail service with Belfast is regretted in commercial circles in Liverpool."

Difficulties with the landing sites were given:

"The aerodrome at Aintree was an exposed place, coupled with which the picking up station at Southport presented many difficulties and brought about much damage to the aeroplanes."

However, local businessmen believed that, "the advantages of the air mail service should have merited a longer trial period to allow teething problems to be addressed." Liverpool's loss was Glasgow's gain and the *Herald* contended that the Scottish city, "will probably take upon itself the title of the air gateway to the North." The following day it reported that the initial flight from Renfrew to Malone, in a de Havilland aircraft carrying the Company's Sales manager FEN St Barbe, had taken place in excellent weather with no difficulties en-route.

On June 26, the *Glasgow Herald* reported:

> "As a result of the survey it was decided to start a service provided that arrangements could be made to have a regular supply of weather reports from various points on this route. Provision has now been made for this and reports are to be collected from Renfrew, Turnberry, Portpatrick, Donaghadee and Belfast. In the first instance one flight will be made in each direction a day. An aeroplane carrying morning newspapers for Belfast will leave Renfrew Aerodrome at about 7.15am and flying by way of Kilburnie to Irvine will follow the coastline of Ayrshire and Wigtownshire to Portpatrick, from which point it will cross the Irish Channel to Belfast, arriving at Malone Aerodrome in about an hour and a quarter. On the return journey, during the summer at least, the aeroplane will leave Belfast about 5pm, carrying mails in addition to three or four passengers."

Regrettably, the Renfrew-Malone link never developed as envisaged.

As an example of the way in which air transport was becoming more reliable, *Flight* Magazine noted on July 31, 1924:

> "By way of an illustration of the work done by the de Havilland

Hire Service, it may be mentioned that on Thursday of last week (July 24) Mr Cobham, flying one of the new DH50 machines, with a Siddeley Puma engine, carried press photographs of the Duke of York's visit to Ireland. Leaving Londonderry at 1.40pm, the machine arrived at Stag Lane aerodrome at 5pm, having covered a distance of 440 miles in three hours 20 minutes. Actually, Cobham was flying at cruising speed, and the surprisingly good time made was the result of a following wind. Leaving again at 4am the next morning, with about half-a-ton of newspapers, Cobham arrived at Belfast at 8.45am, where a stop of close on half-an-hour was made. Londonderry was reached at 9.45. Later in the day the machine returned to Stag Lane. During something like 1½ days a distance of about 1,500 miles was flown, which is extremely good going."

Services to Carlisle

Following the trial period serving Glasgow, Northern Airlines concluded its operations for the year by starting a connection to

As well as DH50s, Northern Airlines also used the smaller DH9, G-EBJW. (WJ Halland)

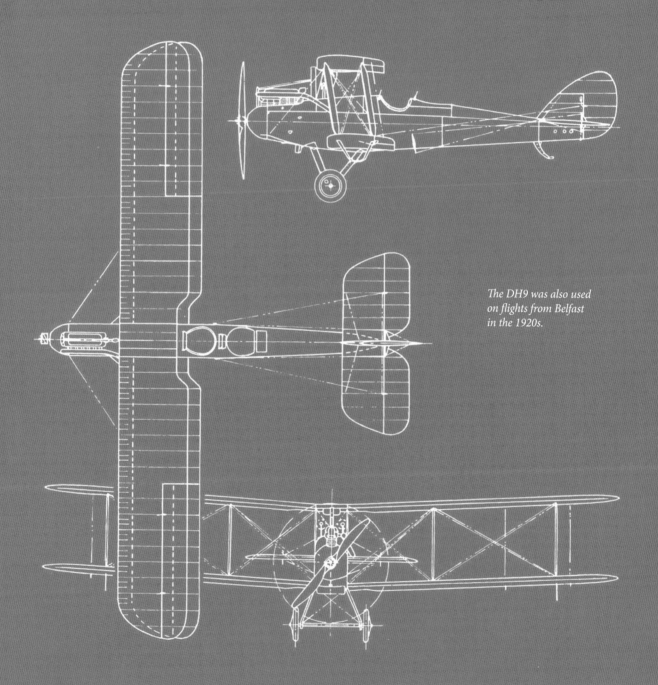

The DH9 was also used on flights from Belfast in the 1920s.

Preparing to refuel a DH50 at a muddy Malone. (Cobham plc)

Carlisle on Tuesday, September 2. The first flight departed Carlisle Swifts airfield at 9am under ideal weather conditions, the three-seater DH9 G-EBJW, powered by a 300hp ADC Nimbus engine and flown by VM Dickinson, crossed the Solway Firth, flew along the Scottish coast as far as Stranraer and made the short crossing to Larne before proceeding to Belfast. In the first instance only mail and newspapers were carried. In July, Messrs Greig and Higgs had visited Carlisle to look for a likely landing site. While they were there, they found the time to win the top prizes in the County Lawn Tennis Tournament – it is hard to imagine an airline executive finding the time, never mind having the ability to perform a similar feat today.

The City Council minutes of October 22 recorded that, "As the service between Belfast and Carlisle had now been established and was in operation every day it was necessary to cinder a portion of the ground which is still soft." The Town Clerk also reported that, "Colonel Outram, representing the Air Ministry, inspected the Aerodrome last week and had expressed himself as satisfied with it subject to the cindering being carried out."

The operation to Carlisle continued until November 3 on a daily basis, when the winter break was taken.

Stranraer and Londonderry

The following year, Northern Airlines tried again and as evidence of the company's intent, an additional DH9 was purchased, G-EBJX. The DH9 was a civilian conversion of the wartime light bomber. Unlike the DH50, these two aircraft did not have an enclosed cabin. Instead two passengers could be carried in open cockpits behind the pilot. Accordingly they would have required helmet, goggles and flying clothing supplied by the airline for the duration of the flight.

Some encouragement had been received over the winter months, in the form of a grant from Belfast City Council of £1700 to help

DH-9 G-EBJX of Northern Airlines. (AJ Jackson Collection)

Dear Sir,

AEROPLANE HANGAR.

I have to inform you that your letter of the 13th instant requesting the Corporation to erect a Hut for Office purposes at the Aerodrome, Gransha, has been referred to the City Surveyor for the purpose of being dealt with.

Yours faithfully,

F. Henry Miller.

Town Clerk.

The Managing Director,
Northern Air Lines Ltd.
47, Foyle Street,
LONDONDERRY.

with operating costs. The Chamber of Commerce in Londonderry also became interested and offered £1000 if a route extension to Derry was agreed. To this end landing rights were granted on February 28, 1925 by the management committee of the asylum, provided that aircraft did not fly within one mile of the institution. The Derry City Council Minutes of April 20, 1925 report a letter received from the Managing Director of Northern Airlines Ltd, Astor House, Aldwych, London WC2, asking for a hangar to be erected on the grounds at Gransha, to the north of the city on the eastern side of the River Foyle. A subsequent letter was directed to an address within the city at 47, Foyle Street, concerning the provision of a hut for office purposes.

Donald Greig was interviewed in the *Belfast Weekly Telegraph* on January 24 and noted:

> "There has been a good response on the part of investors for the £10,000 capital wanted. Had it not been for the support of the Lord Mayor of Belfast, the Town Clerk and the Ministry of Commerce, the project would have been utterly impossible. Three de Havilland machines will be used in the service and in order to avoid long delays through bad weather, Strangford – 45 miles from Belfast – will be used as a calling place. If the conditions are against safe flying the mails can then be re-loaded to a waiting steamer. We shall arrange our schedule to work in conjunction with the train expresses from the two cities."

No further details of the proposed Strangford landing site have been discovered or indeed, any concerning how a steamer would be kept waiting.

The 1925 schedule opened with a newspaper flight from Carlisle to Belfast on March 18. As in the previous year, the weather was a major limiting factor and an effort was made to identify an alternative which would ensure an unbroken service. The *Glasgow Herald* of March 21, 1925 announced that:

> "Trial flights in connection with a daily air mail service between Scotland and Belfast have proved eminently satisfactory. The Scottish terminus is a former Royal Naval Air Service aerodrome at Freugh, near Stranraer, which is only some thirty miles from Ireland. The mail train from London reaches Stranraer about six o'clock each morning and the conveyance of the mails to Belfast by aeroplane instead of the cross-channel steamer will effect a time saving of over

two hours. Two aeroplanes have been purchased for the new service, which has the support of all businessmen."

During the Great War RNAS Luce Bay at Stranraer had been the operating base for coastal patrol airships and had a connection to aviation in Ulster, as in case of unfavourable weather, a mooring-out station with a 150 feet long portable airship shed was set up at Bentra near Whitehead. A regular duty of the airships was to escort the Larne–Stranraer ferry, *Princess Maud*. The full story of this is told in a companion volume to this book: *Airships over Ulster – Royal Naval Air Service Airships during the First World War*.

On March 17 a dummy sack of mail and a consignment of newspapers had been sent to Stranraer on the overnight train. In the early hours of the next morning, this was picked up at the station and brought to East Freugh Farm. The second DH9, G-EBJX, which was to be based at Stranraer, took off at 6.18am and arrived in Belfast some 47 minutes later.

An eyewitness account

Not only the press and the business community were interested, a young boy witnessed an early flight from Malone. At the age of 85, Bob Howe recalled in a letter to the author:

> "When I was about eleven years old and living on the Stranmillis Road, a pal and I heard that for the first time some *Belfast Telegraph*s would be flown across the water from Malone – so the two of us went up in that direction. We could have walked, cycled or gone up in the tram, I just can't remember how we got there. The area is now the Taughmonagh Estate. We went into the fields and got as near as we could to where we saw a reddish, fabric covered,

The Belfast Telegraph *recorded progress at Malone.* (Belfast Telegraph)

single-engine biplane with some fuss going on around it. We lay on our tummies at the bottom of the nearest thorn hedge as close as we could get to the group and I'm quite sure we waited for the take-off. That was about the third week in March 1925."

The official history of the *Belfast Telegraph* records that this flight took place on March 23, 1925. Photographs show two aircraft, one the DH 50, G-EBFN and the other a DH9, G-EBJX, with newspaper delivery vans clustered around. In another, two pilots in long leather coats stand in a small group in front of a DH50 and in a third, the corner of a temporary looking hanger is visible – though given the evidence in the minutes concerning the Air Ministry's inability to supply one, this photograph may well have been taken

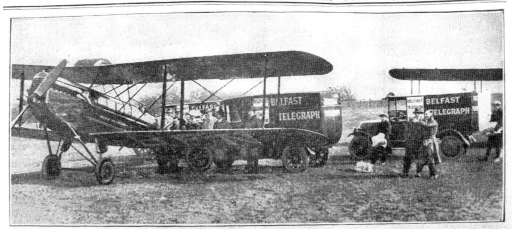

NEWSPAPERS BY AEROPLANE.

COPIES OF THE "BELFAST TELEGRAPH," PRINTED AT FIVE O'CLOCK IN THE AFTERNOON, AND DESPATCHED FROM MALONE, BELFAST, BY AEROPLANE, ARE ON SALE IN SCOTLAND AT SIX O'CLOCK.

One of the photographs on the opposite page as it appeared in the Belfast Telegraph *in 1925. (Belfast Central Newspaper Library)*

elsewhere. Moreover, in a conversation with the author, Bob Howe said that he had no recollection of a hangar at Malone. A caption in the paper stated, "Copies of the *Belfast Telegraph* printed at five o'clock in the afternoon and dispatched from Malone, Belfast by aeroplane are on sale in Scotland at six o'clock."

An advert appearing in the local press in Stranraer on March 31 stated, "News by Aeroplane. The *Belfast Telegraph* is forwarded each evening by aeroplane to Stranraer. On sale about 6.30 by :- Mr William Fleming 25 Hanover Street, Miss Fleming 85 George Street, Miss M'Haffie Hanover Street. Twelve pages. Price, three-halfpence. All the day's sporting and latest news to five o'clock."

All-weather Mac

During 1925, the Chief Pilot of Northern Airlines was Captain RH McIntosh, 'All-weather Mac' (so called after landing at a fogbound

Croydon in the Handley Page O/10 G-EATH on October 20, 1921). He tells his story in his autobiography:

"I now found myself with four months in hand before Imperials would take me back and with a bank balance teetering on the red. I knew Donald Grieg, he made me temporary Chief Pilot. When I travelled up to join the company I found that the main source of income was a contract from the London *Daily Chronicle* to run a regular newspaper service between Stranraer and Belfast. We loaded up and flew them across to Malone aerodrome in plenty of time for the *Chronicle* to beat its competitors by several hours and in three months or so the sales of this paper soared to unexpected heights.

We had Puma-engined DH9s [G-EBDG and G-EBIG] and the larger DH50s. It really wasn't much fun and at times with Atlantic gales and the fogs of the Irish Sea, it was sheer misery. Met forecasts were non-existent. Time and time again on arrival at Malone, the aerodrome would be fog-bound. We then had to circle waiting impatiently for the fog to clear. If it didn't, back across the water we would go to refuel and try again. I once had three weary attempts before I could at last get down on the grass at Malone and deliver my load.

Captain RH McIntosh poses alongside a DH34 of Imperial Airways at Croydon. (via Ann and Brian Stanley)

[Note that there is no mention of Strangford or steamers, perhaps Donald Grieg had been talking a good story to boost business.]

> Even when we eventually landed as late as 10am, we still beat the rival newspapers, for the fog delayed the boats as well. On the trip back, we carried copies of the *Belfast Telegraph* and occasionally a courageous passenger would share the tiny cabin of the DH50, hemmed in by bundles of newspapers. Northern Airlines very nearly got a Post Office contract for mails. One foggy day a pilot dropped the mailbag on fog-bound Malone Aerodrome rather than risk landing. The wretched bag was never found and lost too was the GPO contract. This small airline struggled to keep going and do a useful job; just one more link of experience forged for commercial aviation."

The staff did, however, also have time to consider the possible fringe benefits of their situation, again as RH McIntosh recalls:

> "Malone was just a field next to a golf course. Our manager in Belfast was Andrew Stone who, I think, was involved in the theatre over there. He tried to persuade the golf club to grant NAL staff honorary membership. At first he was unsuccessful – until we stopped returning their stray golf balls."

An untoward incident on April 11 was reported in the *Belfast Weekly Telegraph*:

> "Owing to fog, the aeroplane G-EBFN of Northern Airlines made a forced landing in one of the fields of Mr William Boomer's farm at Knockmore about a mile outside Lisburn on Monday morning. The aircraft was coming from Stranraer to the Malone Aerodrome but the pilot lost his bearings owing to the heavy, low-lying clouds. The landing was a

perfect one. The machine only taxied about 100 yards after touching earth and sustained no damage. The pilot made his way to Lisburn and telephoned headquarters, with the result that mails and papers were conveyed to Belfast by motor, the parcels arriving at the distributing centre well up to time. Fortunately the field in which the landing was made is a large one, so that the pilot should experience no difficulty in taking-off as soon as weather conditions permit."

RH McIntosh had a much more potentially dangerous experience on April 14, 1925. On making a difficult landing at Malone in a hailstorm, the DH9 G-EBJX was lifted by a gust of wind and tossed 50 feet into a hedge, luckily without severe damage. The distinguished and experienced pilot exclaimed that it was the worst route for bad weather he had encountered. Following an equally difficult return flight the next day, the service was suspended. However, a resumption was made and a Special Meeting of the General Purposes Committee, headed naturally by Sir William Turner, visited the aerodrome a year after the first flight on April 29. They were sufficiently enthused to propose the addition of a weighbridge to the airfield's facilities and that a tender of £30 for the sheep grazing rights should be accepted. At about this time Captain McIntosh resumed his career with Imperial Airways.

A timetable of May 18, 1925 gives the following schedule:

Depart: Stranraer 6.30am – arrive: Belfast 7.00am – d. Belfast 7.15am – a. Londonderry 8.15am – d. Londonderry 5.00pm – a. Belfast 6.15pm – d. Belfast 7.30pm – a. Stranraer 8.00pm.

Another unfortunate incident took place, when the DH9 G-EBJX was compelled to make a forced landing at Limavady, when returning to Belfast from Londonderry. The aircraft was

```
        MEETING OF GENERAL PURPOSES COMMITTEE.
        --------------------------------------

                                        29th April, 1925.

Members Present :-
        The Right Hon. the Lord Mayor (Alderman
          Sir W. G. Turner) (chairman);
        The High Sheriff (Councillor Macartney);
        Aldermen Barron, Captain Crichton, Jones,
          McConnell, McMordie, and Nixon;
        Councillor Stewart.

                        ---------

                        The Aerodrome.
        The members present proceeded to the Aerodrome, Malone, and having
inspected the lands, it was
        Moved by Alderman McConnell,
        Seconded by Alderman Nixon, and
        Resolved - That the tender obtained, in response to the advertise-
ment, for the sheep grazing of the lands (viz., £30 for the season ending
1st November) be accepted.



                                        Lord Mayor,
                                        Chairman.
```

dismantled where it landed, brought by road to Belfast, repaired and reassembled. Not long after this, the last service was flown on June 8, 1925. Though it lasted but a brief period, the Londonderry connection is of some significance as the first internal air service in Ireland, pre-dating Hugh Cahill's dream of feeder flights from Galway and Cork to Baldonnel – which in fact resulted in only one trial run. On October 24, 1932, Captain OE Armstrong, in

The DH9 G-EBJX which made a forced landing at Limavady in 1925. (Belfast Telegraph)

the DH83 Fox Moth EI-AAP, of the grandly named Iona National Airlines, flew mail from Galway to connect with the KLM Fokker F.XII, PH-AID, en-route for Berlin via Croydon and Rotterdam. Ten years later, from August 12 to October 30, 1942, Aer Lingus maintained a thrice weekly Dublin–Shannon connection, using DH86 Express Airliners.

The end of a bold effort

Soon the Air Ministry equipment at Malone was transferred to Aldergrove. Northern Airlines bold unsubsidised venture was over. Nearly a decade was to pass before a regular air service would link Northern Ireland with the mainland. The de Havilland aircraft were all single-engine biplanes. Bearing in mind the fairly fragile wood and fabric structure of the aircraft, the distinct possibility of engine failure and the lack of navigational or radio facilities, the sea crossing from England or Scotland to Northern Ireland was not without hazard. The courage of those early pioneers and any intrepid passengers should not be underestimated. Northern Airlines made over 100 scheduled flights to and from Northern Ireland, it was an enterprise that deserved greater government support at the time and is worthy of remembrance as having played a part in paving the way for the world in which we now live and travel by air to all parts of the globe.

The Belfast Book of 1929 described the activities of Northern Airlines at Malone and commented:

> "Success is not often achieved at the first attempt. Now what has happened since? The seaplane has developed and the risk of crossing the Channel has almost if not altogether disappeared. Sir Alan Cobham now urges the seaplane and as the Belfast Harbour Commissioners have recently reclaimed a large tract of slobland which is firm and solid with a level surface, all eyes are turned to this as the site for an aerodrome and the waters immediately adjoining it as the port for seaplanes."

In 1928, a Short Calcutta flying boat, G-EBVH, of Imperial Airways had operated for a few weeks between Liverpool and Belfast Harbour, subsidised by the corporations of the two cities. The cargo on an early flight included the first delivery of Irish eggs to be sold in Liverpool on the day they were laid. *The Belfast Book* continued:

> "The Flying Club of Ulster has been formed in Belfast to be one of the links in the chain of clubs in Great Britain and Ireland."

The North of Ireland Aero Club was founded on September 28, 1928 at the Grand Central Hotel, Belfast.

"No doubt before the next issue of *The Belfast Book* a regular service between Belfast, Liverpool, Glasgow and other ports will be in operation" was the hopeful conclusion.

So the optimism as exemplified by Sir William Turner and his colleagues had not entirely evaporated. The story of Ulster's airports, the people and the airlines which provided the services was only just beginning and has been told in two companion volumes to this history, which cover events at Aldergrove, Sydenham, Newtownards and Nutts Corner, *In the Heart of the City* and *Belfast International Airport – Aviation at Aldergrove since 1918*.

Some loose ends

The two three seater DH9s, G-EBJW and G-EBJX were sold to Air Taxis Ltd of Stag Lane, Edgware in London for the sum of £975.12.2. The DH50 prototype, G-EBFN, went to West Australian Airways in 1926. The other DH50, G-EBFP, became part of the Imperial Airways charter hire fleet at Croydon, until it was sold to the Iraq Petroleum Transport company in 1932. Northern Airlines was formally wound up by Edward Higgs in February 1927. Donald Greig forsook aviation for the brewing trade, eventually becoming the free trade manager of Courage and Barclay Breweries. He served with the RAF Regiment during the Second World War and died in the 1959 at the age of 62. Alan Cobham (1894–1973) was knighted for his record breaking flights around the Empire in another DH50, G-EBFO. He later brought air display flying to all parts of the British Isles in the 1930s and then founded the Flight Refuelling Company, now part of Cobham plc. Wing Commander RH McIntosh completed 45 years of flying with 23,000 hours and 143 types in his logbook. Sir Sefton Brancker (1877–1930) died in the R.101 airship disaster. Lieutenant Colonel

Sir Francis Shelmerdine (1881–1945) rose to the eminent position of Director General of Civil Aviation, a post which he held from 1930–1941. The name Northern Airlines surfaced again briefly at Manchester's Barton aerodrome in 1930, primarily as a joy-riding company, with the DH9Cs, G-EBIG and G-EBDG (which had been on strength briefly in 1925), as well as the DH50 G-EBQI. As for Malone, it reverted to farmland, though in 1933 the City Council received an application from John Sword of Midland and Scottish Air Ferries Ltd (M&S). This airline had been operating a service from Glasgow to Belfast since the end of May and had been granted temporary permission to use Aldergrove. The Council at the same time was being asked to consider the establishment of a municipal aerodrome on reclaimed land belonging to the Harbour Commissioners at Sydenham. The Council gave serious consideration to the proposals made by M&S but with the demise of the airline and the opening of 'The Ards Airport' at Newtownards in 1934, they came to nothing. Subsequent minutes, in 1936 and 1937, record applications to use 'Malone Aerodrome' by CWA Scott's Flying Display Ltd and Aircraft Demonstration Ltd for air displays. Permission in both cases was granted. Sadly, Sir William Turner (1872–1937), the Lord Mayor of Belfast from 1923–1928, did not live to see the opening of Belfast Harbour Airport at Sydenham on March 16, 1938.

The land once occupied by the airfield at Malone is now covered by the Taughmonagh housing estate and no evidence of its past use remains – of a time when, as Charles Grey rightly said, "While others have talked about it Belfast has done it."

Bibliography

Primary Sources

Belfast City Council Minutes: 1923, 1924, 1925, 1933, 1936, 1937

Northern Airlines company records supplied by the Public Records Office, London

Periodicals

Croydon Airport Society Journal, 'All-Weather Mac Recollections', 1985

Flight Magazine: 1923, 1924, 1925

The Aeroplane, 1924

Newspapers

Belfast News Letter

Belfast Telegraph

Belfast Weekly Telegraph

Glasgow Herald

Irish Telegraph

Isle of Man Daily Times

Liverpool Daily Courier

Northern Whig

The Times

Books

Brodie, Malcolm, *The Tele – a History of the Belfast Telegraph*, Blackstaff Press, Belfast: 1995

Byrne, Liam, *History of Aviation in Ireland*, Blackwater Press/Folens, Dublin: 1980

Cobham, Alan, *Skyways*, Nisbet & Co Ltd, London: 1925

Connon, Peter, *An Aeronautical History of the Cumbria, Dumfries and Galloway Region Part 2: 1915–1930*, St Patrick's Press, Penrith: 1984

Corlett, John, *Aviation in Ulster*, Blackstaff Press, Belfast: 1981

Gillies, JD and Wood, JL, *Aviation in Scotland*, Glasgow Branch RACS, Glasgow: 1966

Jackson, AJ, *De Havilland Aircraft since 1909*, Putnam, London: 1987

McIntosh, RH, and Spry-Leverton, J, *All-Weather Mac*, Macmillan, London: 1963

Share, Bernard, The Flight of the Iolar, Gill & Macmillan, Dublin: 1986

Acknowledgments

Thanks to: Tony Brunskill, Peter Connon, Leonard Craig, Ernie Cromie, Colin Cruddas, Ms Breidge Doherty, Neville Doyle, Dermot Francis, Bob Howe, David Huddleston, Iain Hutchison, Roger Jackson, Mrs Pat Jenkins, Walter Love, Eddie McIlwaine, Lawrence Shivers, the staff at the Belfast City Library and the Public Record Office for Northern Ireland.

Grateful thanks are also due to Eason and Son Ltd, Belfast City Council, the Esme Mitchell Trust and the late Lady Mairi Bury for their generous sponsorship of the First Edition of this book. Last but by no means least, thanks as always to my wife, Lynda.

Index

People:

Armstrong, Captain OE 57
Baird Family 24
Bartlett, Major 18
Boomer, William 55
Brancker, Sir Sefton 24, 25, 26, 27, 60
Cahill, Hugh 57
Cobham, Alan 11, 13, 14, 16, 21, 24, 25, 29, 34, 35, 36, 37, 40, 45, 59, 60
Curzon, Viscount 42
Dickinson, Capt. VM 40, 47
Dixon, Sir Thomas 24, 25
Douglas, Lieut. Col. Sholto 7
Duff, James 22, 25, 26, 36, 37
Eason & Son Ltd 15, 23, 35, 41
Ferguson, Harry 24
Fleming, Miss 53
Fleming, William 53
Gerrard, Brigadier Gen. EL 9
Greig, Captain Donald 20, 21, 25, 47, 50, 54, 55, 60
Grey, Charles 37, 39, 41, 61
Henderson, Lieut. Colonel GLP 40
Herne, Captain EDC 9
Higgs, Edward 21, 47, 60
HM King George V 9, 31
HM Queen Mary 9
HRH the Duke of York 45
Hope, Captain Walter 16, 18
Horwood, Mr 41
Howe, Bob 51, 53
Ingram, Sarah 35, 37
Irvine, Elsie 12
Leach, William 42
Leslie, Major 9
Londonderry, Marquis of 24

M'Cracken, Mr 35
M'Haffie, Miss 53
McIntosh, Capt. RH 53, 54, 55, 56, 60
McLaurin, Hugh 25, 29
Maturin, Reverend HG 36, 37
Milan, Councillor 36
Moneypenny, Sir Frederick 18
Outram, Colonel 47
Pollock, HM 25
Russell, AO 9
Saint, Captain HJ 21
St Barbe, FEN 44
Salvidge, Sir Archibald 29
Scott, CWA 61
Seely, Major General JEB 8
Shelmerdine, Lieut. Colonel Francis 16, 18, 35, 61
Smith, Noel 16
Stephens, Laura 11
Stephens, Solomon 12
Stone, Andrew 9, 12, 55
Sword, John 61
Thompson, John 22
Turner, Sir William 13, 14, 24, 25, 27, 29, 30, 31, 34, 56, 60, 61
Willis, Archibald 22, 42
Workman, Captain F 9

Places:

Aintree Airfield 24, 29, 30, 39, 43
Aldergrove 7, 10, 11, 12, 13, 15, 16, 41, 58, 61
Alexandra Park 18
Ards Airport 61
Baldonnel Airfield 57
Balmoral 16

Barrow 30, 36
Belfast 8, 9, 12, 13, 14, 16, 23, 30, 31, 32, 34, 36, 38, 39, 41, 42, 43, 47, 50, 54, 56, 59, 60, 61
Belfast Harbour Airport 61
Birmingham 13
Blackpool 36
Bournemouth 21
Castlereagh Road 20
Carlisle 45, 47, 50
Cork 57
Cricklewood Airfield 7
Croydon Aerodrome 54, 58, 60
Donaghadee 30, 36, 44
Drummore 35, 36
Dublin 38, 58
Fleetwood 30
Freugh 50, 51
Galway 57, 58
Glasgow 42, 44, 45, 60, 61
Gransha 49
Hendon Airfield 21
Knockmore 55
Larne 47, 51
Limavady 56
Lisburn 56
Lisburn Road 38, 41
Liverpool 23, 25, 30, 31, 32, 34, 36, 38, 39, 40, 41, 42, 43, 44, 59, 60
London 49
Londonderry 45, 48, 49, 56, 57
Malone Airfield 24, 25, 27, 28, 32, 33, 38, 41, 43, 44, 47, 51, 52, 53, 54, 55, 56, 57, 59, 61
Malone Road 20, 38
Manchester 13, 14, 16, 18, 61

Maryport 36
Musgrave Park 16
Plymouth 13, 16
Portpatrick 44
Portsmouth 21
Renfrew Airfield 42, 44
Shotwick 39
Southport 30, 39, 43
Stag Lane Airfield 45, 60
Strangford 50, 55
Stranmillis Road 51
Stranraer 47, 48, 50, 51, 53, 54, 55, 56
Taughmonagh 51, 61
Turnberry 44
Whitehaven 36
Workington 30, 36

Aircraft:

Avro 504 9
Avro 548 8, 9, 10
Blackburn Kangaroo 7
DH4 7, 10
DH9 7, 10, 14, 15, 21, 45, 46, 47, 48, 51, 52, 54, 56, 60, 61
DH16 7, 10, 11
DH34 18, 54
DH50 11, 12, 13, 16, 17, 24, 26, 27, 28, 31, 32, 39, 43, 45, 47, 48, 49, 52, 54, 55, 60, 61
DH83 58
DH86 58
Fokker F.XII 58
Handley Page O/10 54
Handley Page O/400 7
R.101 60
Short Calcutta 59

If you enjoyed reading this book, then these other publications may also be of interest.

Airships over Ulster
Royal Naval Air Service Airships
during the First World War
Guy Warner £7.99

The Last Canberra – PR9 XH131
Guy Warner £11.25

Lilian Bland
The first woman in the world to
design, build & fly an aeroplane
Guy Warner £5.95

**Bail Out! – Escaping Occupied
France with the Resistance**
Alfie Martin £7.99

Flying From Derry
Eglinton & Naval Aviation in NI
Guy Warner £9.95

Shorts – The Foreman Years
Guy Warner £10 hbk

**Available to buy online at www.booksni.com
or telephone 028 9182 0505**

If this book has encouraged you to take a deeper interest in
aviation in Northern Ireland, past and present, you may wish to
join the **Ulster Aviation Society**. You can explore the information,
history, events and aircraft owned by the society at:

www.ulsteraviationsociety.org